WATCHING NATURE

THE
LIVING
TREE

Nigel Hester

FRANKLIN WATTS
New York/London/Sydney/Toronto

© Franklin Watts 1990

Franklin Watts Inc
387 Park Avenue South
New York
NY 10016

Franklin Watts
96 Leonard Street
London EC2A 4RH

Editor: Su Swallow
Design: K and Co

Illustrations:
Angela Owen, Ron Haywood
Phototypeset by Lineage Ltd, Watford
Printed in Belgium

Photography: Nigel Hester

Additional photography: Biofotos/
Heather Angel 10bc, 16br, 17br, 20bl;
Biofotos/G Kinns 16bl; Biofotos/
J Thomas 17tr; Bruce Coleman/N Black
26tl; Eric and David Hosking 15bl, 24t,
26br; NHPA/Laurie Campbell 9bl;
NHPA/N A Callow 11cl; Survival
Anglia/J Foott 15br; Survival Anglia/
D Green 15bc; Survival Anglia/M Tibbles
27l; Survival Anglia/M Wilding 21;
Barrie Watts 8bc, 8br, 10bl, 17tl; ZEFA
5b, 8bl, 20tr, 23b, 28t, 28b, 29t, 29b.

Front Cover: Zefa

Library of Congress Cataloging-in-Publication Data
Hester, Nigel S.
    The living tree / Nigel Hester.
        p.   cm. — (Watching nature)
    Summary: Examines the parts of a tree and its life cycle from
seedling to decay.
    ISBN 0-531-14007-5
    1. Trees—Juvenile literature.   2. Trees—Life cycles—Juvenile
literature.   [1. Trees.] I. Title. II. Series.
QK475.8.H47   1990   89-38997
582.16—dc20   CIP AC

CONTENTS

WHAT KIND OF TREE?

Can you see a tree from where you are, or picture one that grows near your house or school? What do you know about your tree? Think about its shape and about its leaves. Have you ever noticed flowers or nuts on it? Do any animals live in your tree? This book tells you some of the things to look out for when you are near trees.

All trees are either deciduous or evergreen. A deciduous tree sheds all its leaves once every year, usually in the autumn. Most deciduous trees have broad, flat leaves.

Evergreen trees are covered in leaves all the time, although the leaves do drop off all through the year. Most evergreen trees have leaves like needles. Most conifers, such as firs, pines and cedars, are evergreen with needles. A few evergreen trees, such as the holly, are broad-leaved.

Shape and type

This oak has plenty of room to grow and it is easy to see its rounded shape. Notice its wide, strong trunk and spreading branches.

The poplar grows tall and slender, and its branches all point upwards. In France poplars are planted along roads as windbreaks.

Shape and position

A Scotch pine growing on open hill country has a flat top. Its branches are often gnarled and twisted. It is easy to recognise this tree by its shape when it has plenty of room to grow.

These Scotch pines have much less room in a plantation. They are more narrow and upright. The lower branches have lost their needles, and will die back.

Trees that grow near the coast are often shaped by the wind. These larches are leaning away from the sea because they stand in the way of the wind blowing in off the sea.

▷ The holly is an evergreen tree or shrub. Its leaves are shiny, with spines along the edges. Old or shaded holly trees often have only one spine on each leaf, at the tip. In the past, holly was cut and fed to farm animals.

Each type of tree has its own shape. An oak looks quite different from a poplar, and neither of them looks like a Scotch pine. Tree shapes also depend on the place where a tree grows and on the weather. An oak in a field has plenty of sunlight, so it will spread its branches wide. An oak in a wood has to compete with other trees and grows higher to reach the light.

TRUNKS AND ROOTS

The trunk of a tree grows stout and rigid to support its load of branches and leaves. Trees growing in open spaces have much broader trunks than trees in woodland, because they have more leaves to hold up.

The tough layer of bark keeps the trunk from drying out in the sun and wind. On some trees, the bark protects them against damage from forest fires. On others, it keeps out harmful fungi and insects.

Tree roots grow as the tree grows, spreading out sideways to anchor the plant in the ground. The fine hairs along the roots absorb water from the soil. At the tip of each root is a tough, hard root cap, which protects the growing point.

△ The Douglas fir has a tall, straight trunk. It grows quickly and can reach 75 feet in just 25 years. It can grow to 325 feet, but the tallest trees in the world are probably the Pacific coastal redwoods, which can be up to 360 feet high.

◁ You may be able to study the roots of a tree blown down in a storm.

Oak bark has deep grooves

White birch bark is papery and silver-white

Scotch pine and other conifer tree bark cracks open with age, leaving raised plates

Did you know...?

Oak bark contains a chemical called tannin, which is used to make animal skins into leather. Birch bark was used by some North American Indians to make the "skin" of their canoes.

The bark of Scotch pine, like most conifer bark, produces gum. If the tree is cut, or if the bark cracks open, the gum leaks out to seal the wound.

Finding out

A tree can be identified just from the pattern and texture of its bark. A useful way to study bark is to make rubbings. Attach waxed or greaseproof paper to the trunk with sticky tape. Rub firmly but slowly with a wax crayon. Keep the crayon fairly flat so the paper does not tear.

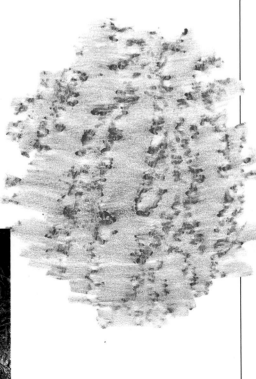

Trees, like all plants, need sunlight in order to grow. They absorb in sunlight through their leaves, which are like little factories making food for the tree. The leaves contain chlorophyll, which uses energy from the sunlight to turn carbon dioxide and water into simple sugar. This process is called photosynthesis.

Broad-leaved trees have either simple or compound leaves. The oak has simple leaves: each leaf has its own stalk. The ash has compound leaves, where each leaf is divided into several leaflets attached to one stem. Conifers have leaves shaped like needles.

A food factory

During the day, when it is light, the leaves of a tree are busy making food by a process called photosynthesis. The food is a simple sugar, which is sent to other parts of the tree to make it grow.

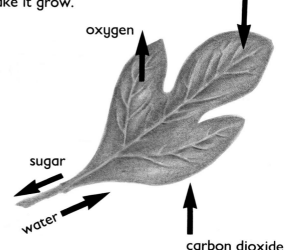

sunlight

oxygen

sugar

water

carbon dioxide

The life of a leaf

Buds of broad-leaved trees form on the sides of branches and at the top of twigs. They start to grow in the autumn, even before the old leaves fall. The buds are protected through the winter by tough scales, which burst open in spring as the buds swell. The leaves unfold and spread out so that as many as possible are in the sun. When the leaves die and fall, they leave a scar where they were attached to the tree.

The horse chestnut: buds

leaves

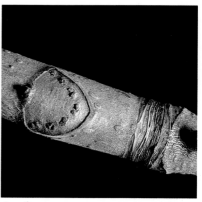

leaf scar

Simple leaves

The oak has lobed leaves.

Young beech leaves are hairy.

The elm has toothed leaves.

Compound leaves

The ash has pairs of leaflets.

The horse chestnut leaflets look like the fingers of a hand.

The mountain ash has toothed leaflets.

Conifer leaves

The needles of the Scotch pine are blue-green and slightly twisted. They grow in pairs.

Larch needles grow in bunches of 30 or more. They fall in autumn.

The flat needles of the yew are arranged all around the twig.

All broad-leaved trees have flowers and most trees have both male and female flowers on the same plant. Pollen from the male flowers has to be transferred to the female flowers so that seeds can be made. Most trees rely on wind to blow the pollen from one flower to the other. But wind pollination is not very reliable, so large amounts of pollen are produced. A single birch catkin can release more than five million grains of pollen.

Conifers do not have true flowers; they have male and female cones instead. The male cones produce pollen like male flowers.

▷ After pollination the female cone grows. When it is ripe, like this Douglas fir cone, it opens and sheds its seeds.

▷ Some tree flowers are pollinated by insects which visit the flowers to collect nectar. The pollen sticks to their bodies and is carried to another flower. The horse chestnut is pollinated by bees.

▽ The hazel is one of the first trees to come into flower in the spring. The male flowers, called catkins, start to grow in the autumn, when they are brown. In the spring they turn yellow. The catkins, also called lambs' tails because of their shape, release their pollen into the air. The wind carries the tiny grains, and some stick to the little red female flowers growing along the twig *(inset)*.

▽ The oak produces nuts called acorns. Each nut is a single seed in a hard shell. The cup is made from special leaves called bracts. The triangular nuts, or mast, of the beech grow in hairy husks *(below right)*.

▷ The hawthorn grows as a small tree or shrub. It has clusters of small white flowers in May, which are pollinated by insects. Birds feed on its red berries in autumn and winter.

Did you know...?

Some broad-leaved trees produce seeds with wings. Winged seeds travel further than other seeds, so they are more likely to find open ground with plenty of light. The maple seed is the most efficient of all because of the design of its winged case.

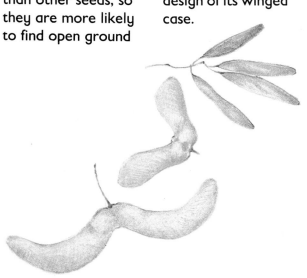

After pollination, the female flowers of broad-leaved trees produce seeds. Some seeds form inside brightly colored fruit or berries. Birds that feed on the fruit scatter the seeds in their droppings, and new trees may grow where the seeds fall.

Some trees produce seeds in the form of nuts. Squirrels and other animals feed on the nuts, but any that they drop may take root and grow. Trees like the ash and maple have seeds in a winged case. The wings help the seeds to be carried on the wind. With luck, some will land in a suitable place to germinate and grow into new trees.

Trees grow quickest in the spring. The tips of a tree's shoots push outwards, and its roots push down into the soil. The trunk gets thicker as a band of new wood forms under the bark. This wood is pale. During the summer the tree grows more slowly. A band of darker wood is formed in the trunk. Two bands of wood, one pale and one dark, are formed each year. They are known as annual rings.

Apart from giving support to the tree, the trunk transports water and food. Water is drawn up into the trunk from the ground by the roots. Sugar made in the leaves passes down the trunk.

Did you know...?

 Oaks do not usually produce acorns until they are about 50 years old.

 A medium-sized oak takes in up to 630 liters of water a day.

 The oak produces up to 50,000 acorns in a bumper year.

 The oldest oak on record was at least 1500 years old.

 A single oak can support nearly 300 different kinds of insects.

 A mature oak sheds about a quarter of a million leaves every autumn.

 Oak boughs often grow in a zig-zag pattern.

 Many parks were once planted with oaks to provide timber for building ships for the navy.

 Oaks are struck by lightning more often than many other trees. This is partly because they are tall trees which often stand alone in open spaces.

Looking at the rings of a tree is a bit little like being a detective looking for clues. The thickness of the rings tells you about the history of the tree.

Very narrow rings mean very little growth – perhaps there was a drought that year. A dark scar can be a sign of a forest fire in the past.

Measuring a tree

How old is the tree?

By measuring the girth of a tree, you can figure out how old it is without cutting it down. Measure around the trunk about 5 feet above the ground. In open ground, a tree trunk grows almost one inch a year. So a girth of 100 inches will roughly equal 100 years. In a dense wood a tree may only grow by one half inch a year.

▷ These children are measuring the girth of a tree.

▽ These children are measuring the height of a tree.

How tall is the tree?

A forester uses a special instrument to measure the height of a tree. But you can find out roughly how tall a tree is very simply. Starting at the base of the trunk, walk away from the tree. Every pace or so, stop and bend down, looking back between your legs. When you are just able to see the top of the tree, stand still. The distance from that point back to the base of the trunk roughly equals the height of the tree.

▽ When you can see the top of the tree between your legs, you can figure out its height.

A large tree is like a three-story house, with different kinds of animals living on each floor. The leafy top "floor" of a tree, called the canopy, is home to many insects and birds. Few plants grow in the canopy because it is too dry up there.

Trees native to the United States support the greatest variety of wildlife. Over the centuries, plants and animals have adapted themselves to these trees and depend on them for a home. Trees that have been introduced from other countries have much less wildlife living in them.

△ The canopy of native trees provides food and shelter for many animals, especially birds and insects. The leafy branches give protection against predators and severe weather, and a support for nests.

These larches *(inset)* are not native trees. They provide a home for fewer than 20 kinds of insect and do not attract many birds.

Trees that support a large number of insects attract a wide variety of insect-eating birds. Flycatchers feeds mainly in the canopy, catching flying insects on the wing. The chickadee tit often searches for food in small flocks. Fewer birds are found in conifers than in broad-leaved trees because food is scarce.

Some birds build their nests in the canopy, where they are safe from most predators.

▽ The flycatcher and chickadee tit nest in trees and feed mainly on insects. The siskin nests in conifers and eats the seeds of pine and spruce.

▷ The heron is one of the largest birds to nest in a tree. The tree must be close to water so that the parent birds can catch fish for their young.

flycatcher

long-tailed tit

siskin

The gray squirrel is a common sight in the canopy of oak, beech and sycamore woods. It feeds mainly on the buds, flowers and fruits of the trees. The squirrel's greatest enemy is man, because of the damage it can cause to forestry plantations. Squirrels like stripping off the bark of young trees, and the trees die. The squirrels are seen as pests and so some are killed.

Apart from mistletoe, few plants can cope with the dry conditions in the canopy of a tree. Lichens, which are simple plants, grow on trees where the air is not polluted.

▽ Mistletoe usually grows on oaks and poplars. It is a semi-parasite: it takes water and some of its food from its host tree. Thrushes like to eat its white berries.

▽ This beard lichen hangs from branches of oak and ash. Unlike most lichens, it does not mind direct sunlight, but it needs moist, clean air. Birds use this lichen as nesting material.

◁ The squirrel can run up and down the smoothest tree trunks. It builds its nest high in a broad-leaved tree. Old nests *(below)* are easy to see in winter when the trees are bare.

◁ The vapourer moth caterpillar is easy to spot on trees or bushes. Its vivid markings and 'shaving brush' tufts help to stop birds eating it.

Many of the insects that are found in broad-leaved trees are leaf-eaters. More than 100 kinds of moth caterpillars feed on the leaves and buds of oak. High in the canopy, these caterpillars munch on the foliage all through the summer. Trees are sometimes stripped bare. Without its covering of leaves, an oak cannot produce food, so it grows a second crop of leaves.

Other insects in the canopy are less harmful. The purple hairstreak butterfly, for example, lays its eggs on twigs and feeds on the honeydew produced by aphids.

△ The purple hairstreak butterfly is difficult to spot as it stays high in the canopy of oaks.

▽ Tiny gall wasps lay their eggs inside the leaves and buds of trees. Growths form like these cherry galls. The young larvae feed on the inside of the gall.

The trunk of a tree supports its own group of animals and plants which make their home halfway up the tree, between the canopy and the ground.

Many insects live in the cracks and crevices of the bark. They travel up and down the trunk to find food or to look for a place to lay eggs. A few insects are like highwaymen, waiting to pounce on the traveling insects.

Most of this activity takes place at night. In the day, it is dangerous to be out in the open because of the birds. Even at night the insects are at risk. Spiders in particular hunt their prey during the dark hours. Some spin a web, others stalk their prey.

The trunk of a tree supports a surprising variety of animals and plants.

Woodlice live in leaf litter. They venture up the trunk at night to feed on lichens, but they may be caught on the way by a spider, owl or shrew.

The great ground beetle travels up the trunk to hunt for caterpillars among the leaves. Other beetles feed beneath the bark.

The wood wasp is not a true wasp, but a type of sawfly. The female lays its eggs deep in the trunks of conifers. The larvae live inside the trunk for many years.

Did you know...?

The bark of many trees is used in industry. The para rubber tree, which grows in South America, contains latex, which can be made into rubber. When cuts are made in the bark, the latex flows out and is collected.

The bark of the cork oak, which grows in southern Europe, provides cork for floor tiles, bottle corks and so on. The bark is stripped off every few years, during which time a new layer grows.

The pale form of the peppered moth is well camouflaged on lichen-covered bark. The dark form is well hidden on dirty buildings.

Many kinds of lichens, mosses and ferns grow on the main trunk, as well as in the canopy. The fork between the trunk and the branches is a collecting place for bird droppings and other material. This provides the food for certain plants to develop, although few of them are flowering plants. Some fungi also thrive in this shady part of the tree. They develop from spores (like seeds) blown by the wind, which lodge in cracks in the bark.

If there is plenty of light around the tree, then some flowering plants are able to climb up the tree trunk. They use the trunk for support to enable them to reach the light.

Ivy clings to the trunk with sticky pads on small roots. It does not flower until it reaches the light. Bees and other insects are attracted by its nectar.

Some lichens cover the trunk so densely that it is hard to see the bark. This one, with its bright red fruiting patches, only grows in very ancient woodland sites.

Honeysuckle twines around young trees so tightly that it distorts or even kills them. The sweet-smelling nectar of its flowers attracts night-flying hawkmoths.

The tree trunk provides a feeding ground for a wide variety of birds. The birds move up and down the trunk in search of insects, eggs and larvae hidden in cracks and under the bark. Some small birds are well adapted to life on the trunk. The nuthatch can walk down the trunk as well as up. The brown creeper moves around the trunk in a spiral, clinging to the bark with its long, sharp claws and using its stiff tail as a prop.

Small and large birds nest in holes in tree trunks. Woodpeckers make a hole by tapping away at the wood with their sharp beaks. Owls look for old, hollow trees in which to nest.

△ The woodpecker makes a nesting hole in a tree trunk. It feeds on insects such as carpenter ants on the woodland floor.

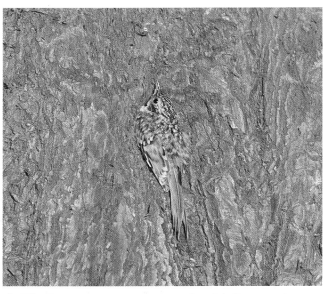

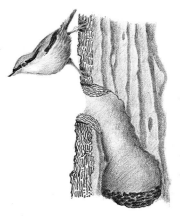

△ The brown creeper scrapes away soft wood with its beak to make a little hollow away from the wind and cold. It nests in a crack in the tree or under a loose flap of bark.

△ The nuthatch nests in a hole in a tree trunk. It lines the nest with a bed flakes of bark, feathers, grass, hair and roots.

▷ The barred owl nests in a hole in the trunk. If it cannot find a hole it may use an old squirrel or crow's nest in the canopy.

The base of the tree trunk is the ground floor of our three-story tree house. In deciduous woods large numbers of small creatures live in the leaf litter – the layer of dead leaves under a tree. Some of the animals, such as mites, are too tiny to be seen, but they feed on the leaves and help to rot them down. Millipedes, worms and ants also feed on leaf material. Centipedes, beetles, spiders and other small predators hunt tiny animals among the dark, damp leaf litter.

Small mammals search the ground under trees for seeds, fruit and nuts to eat. They are shy animals, but they often leave clues such as nibbled cones and nutshells.

Some fungi live at the base of a tree, taking their food from the tree roots or the leaf litter.

The leaf litter in conifer woods supports less wildlife than the leaf litter of broad-leaved woods. The fallen needles take many years to decay and do not provide a suitable habitat for many flowers or animals.

Detective work

Look on the ground under trees for clues about animals that have visited the tree.

Squirrels gnaw away the scales on cones to feed on the seeds. Look for rough cone stems left under conifers.

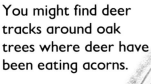

Piles of pips near mountain ash, holly or hawthorn probably mean that birds have been feeding on the tree berries.

You might find deer tracks around oak trees where deer have been eating acorns.

Empty nutshells may have been left by a mouse. Look for teeth marks on the shells.

△ The violet ground beetle is one of the largest insects to be found in the leaf litter. It has powerful jaws for catching its prey.

The giant black slug *(above right)* is common in broad-leaved woods. It is often hidden in damp leaves or hollows. It feeds on fungi.

▷ The deer mouse feeds on tree seeds, fruits and nuts. It stores seeds for the winter, hiding them in the ground.

△ The brightly colored fly agaric is a common sight under birches. It is poisonous. The false death cap *(left)* grows in oak and beech woods. It could be mistaken for the real death cap, which is deadly. The large cauliflower, or brain fungus *(below)* is found in conifer woods.

Under the ground

If you could dig a cross section through the soil under a tree, you would find a dark world of tunnels and roots. Chipmunks and rabbits often burrow under woodland trees, whose roots help to support their underground homes. Smaller mammals such as voles, shrews and deer mice may burrow and nest under hedges. Some burrowing animals store food underground, too.

Worms feed on dead plant material and some pull fallen leaves down into the ground. The leaves rot away and help enrich the soil around the tree roots. Worm tunnels help water to drain through the soil, and allow air to reach the roots of the tree.

The soil is also alive with all kinds of smaller creatures, some of them too small to be seen without a microscope. Some insects lay their eggs in the soil, where the young larvae remain until they reach the adult stage.

▷ The roots of the tree provide shelter and food for a large variety of animals and insects.

skunk

fungi

The skunk and the meadow vole both dig a number of entrance and exit holes to their underground homes. The meadow vole comes out to feed in the day, but the skunk is also active at night.

worms

meadow vole

Worms and other small creatures in the soil help to break down the leaf litter that lies under a tree. The roots of fungi also feed on decaying plant material.

periodic cicadas

The periodic cicadas live underground for two to twenty years before emerging as adult beetles. The fat white grubs damage plants by feeding on their roots.

In prehistoric times, before man, America was carpeted with forests. When trees died and fell, the decaying wood provided a different kind of habitat. All kinds of plants and animals evolved to make use of this habitat. Sadly, much of our woodland has now gone, and the deadwood habitat is threatened.

Fungi play an important role in the decaying process of deadwood. The threads of fungi push through to the center of a stump, taking food from the wood and causing it to rot from the inside outward. The larger fungi appear first, when there are still enough nutrients in the wood to support them. Other, smaller fungi then invade the wood.

As trees get old, they are more

◁ The velvet shank fungus is slimy, apart from its velvety stem. Most fungi die in early winter frosts, but the velvet shank often survives until spring, unless the weather is very cold.

▽ As the stump begins to decay, mosses are able to gain a foothold. Wood sorrel is a common flower on old tree stumps.

△ Many other small creatures, like these snails, also live on deadwood.

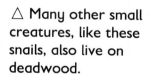

▷ Among the first insects to move into an old stump are the small wood-boring beetles. Not long after, larger beetles lay their eggs in the rotting wood. The stag beetle is America's largest beetle.

and more at risk from disease and attack by pests. Quite often the central wood of the tree decays completely, leaving a hollow trunk. Ancient oak and ash can continue to live for many years with hollow centers. Birds, mice, bats and squirrels use dry hollows in trees for shelter and nesting.

Small hollows can occur in trees for a number of reasons. A fungus may rot part of the tree. Lightning can damage the tree and cause openings. Even the way in which some boughs twist and turn can create hollows. Some mosquitoes and other insects breed only in wet tree hollows, where their larvae are safe from predators that live in larger areas of water.

▷ This ancient oak is still alive, although its center has rotted away because of disease. The long-eared bat (*above*) roosts in hollow trunks. All bats are beneficial and should not be disturbed in any way.

Deciduous trees, like this maple, change with the seasons. You could follow the life of a broad-leaved, deciduous tree near your home and perhaps keep a diary through the year.

In spring, flowers under trees bloom before the tree leaves block out the light. Deer nibble the tree's new shoots and strip the bark as they rub the velvet off their new antlers. Birds build their nests.

In summer, the birds are busy catching insects to feed their chicks. Young birds make short flights from their tree nests as they learn to fly. Bats circle trees to catch insects. On hot days farm animals move to the shade under trees. There is little plant growth under the tree because there is not enough light.

In autumn, the tree leaves change color and begin to fall. Birds feed on the berries and nuts. Small mammals store fallen fruits for the winter, hiding them in the leaf litter or in the soil. Owls are active, hunting the small mammals feeding around trees. In damp weather fungi appear.

In winter, little groups of wrens, which usually live alone, shelter together in tree holes. Flocks of cardinals and chickadees feed on tree fruits. Blackbirds, robins and sparrows dig in the leaf litter for worms and small insects. Squirrels return to the tree to search for the nuts which they buried in the autumn.

Scotch pine

oak

mountain ash

beech

ash

yew

hazel

maple

horse chestnut

European larch

hawthorn

Lombardy poplar

holly

birch

elm

sweet chestnut

SPOT THE LEAF
Now that you have read about trees, test your knowledge and see if you can identify the sixteen leaves which have been scattered at the top of some of the pages in this book. You will find the answers to the quiz below.

Page 1, maple, p 2 European larch, p 3 ash, p 5 horse chestnut, p 7 elm, p 9 beech, p 11 rowan, p 13 yew, p 15 Scotch pine, p 17 silver birch, p 19 hazel, p 20 hawthorn, p 23 sweet chestnut, p 24 oak, p 27 holly, p 29 Lombardy poplar.

PRINTED IN BELGIUM BY

proost
INTERNATIONAL BOOK PRODUCTION